COPYRIGHT© 2010-2025 J

No part of this material may be re[produced]
mechanical, including photocopyi[ng]
without express written, dated, and signed permission from the [author/publisher]

Disclaimer and/or Legal Notices:

The information contained in this publication is provided for educational and informational purposes only. While the Author and Publisher have made every effort to ensure accuracy and safety, they assume no responsibility for errors, omissions, or outcomes resulting from the use of the information provided.

This book presents ideas, recipes, and techniques for creating long-term, shelf-stable meals using dry canning, dehydration, vacuum sealing, and similar preservation methods. These practices are commonly used in survival preparation, emergency planning, and home food storage. However, individual results may vary based on ingredients, equipment, storage conditions, and adherence to safety guidelines.

This publication is not a substitute for professional advice from food safety experts or government agencies. Readers are strongly encouraged to consult current guidelines from the USDA, the FDA, or the National Center for Home Food Preservation to ensure that any food preservation methods used are safe and suitable for their environment and health circumstances.

The Author and Publisher do not make any representations or warranties with respect to the nutritional value, shelf life, or safety of the preserved meals if not properly stored or prepared. Readers assume full responsibility for their choices and practices.

Any references to emergency preparedness, survival situations, or long-term food independence are included as part of a broader discussion on self-reliance and do not imply a guarantee of safety or longevity of stored food.

By reading this book, the Purchaser or Reader acknowledges and accepts all risks associated with food preservation and long-term storage, and agrees to use their own judgment, consult experts where appropriate, and follow all applicable food safety practices and regulations.

Introduction 3
Chapter 1: The Basics of Meals in a Jar 5
Chapter 2: Essential Equipment and Supplies 8
Chapter 3: Choosing and Preparing Ingredients 11
Chapter 4: Step-by-Step Jar Meal Preparation 14
Chapter 5: Breakfasts 17
Chapter 6: Lunches 23
Chapter 7: Dinners 29
Chapter 8: Snacks 37
Chapter 9: Desserts 43
Chapter 10: Advanced Tips and Tricks 49
Chapter 11: Meal Planning and Organization 51
Chapter 12: Frequently Asked Questions 54
Conclusion: One Jar at a Time 57

INTRODUCTION

It started with a storm. One of those late-autumn blizzards that rolls in out of nowhere and knocks the power out for a week. We had two little ones bundled in quilts, a pantry that was full (but not practical), and a realization that changed everything: we weren't as prepared as we thought we were.

That was over a decade ago. Since then, I've made it my mission to ensure that no matter what life throws our way — be it a power outage, job loss, or just a day too busy to cook — we have nourishing, complete meals ready to go. Meals that I trust. Meals that taste like home.

That's where *meals in a jar* come in.

These aren't just convenience foods. They're a testament to old-fashioned wisdom blended with modern preparedness. Every jar I put on the shelf is a promise to my family: *You'll be fed. You'll be safe. We're ready.*

The Blessing of Shelf-Stable Suppers

Meals in a jar are shelf-stable for up to 25 years — yes, you read that right — when done properly. But even more than their longevity, it's the peace of mind they bring that matters most. Whether we're dealing with a crisis or simply need a break from scratch cooking, I can pull a jar from the pantry, add boiling water, and serve something hot and homemade.

These jars have seen us through hard winters, long canning seasons, and even helped Dan out in the shop when he's too busy to stop for a proper lunch. They're a blessing on busy days and a lifeline in emergencies.

Who This Book Is For

If you're here, chances are you already feel the tug to live more intentionally. Maybe you're a homesteader like me, elbow-deep in compost and canning lids. Maybe you're just getting started with prepping or looking for a way to make real food last longer. Either way, this book is for you. It's for:

- Homesteaders who want real food independence.
- Preppers who want long-term peace of mind.
- Moms (and dads!) trying to stretch every dollar while feeding their families well.
- Grandparents who want to leave a legacy of preparedness and provision.

You don't need a fancy setup. You don't need a solar-powered bunker. You just need jars, the right know-how, and a little grit.

What You'll Learn

Over these pages, I'll walk you through everything I've learned — the hard way and the blessed way. You'll learn:

- What tools and ingredients to invest in (and which ones I regret buying).
- How to build nutritionally complete meals your family *will actually eat*.
- My favorite 50+ recipes — real family food, not just survival mush.
- How to label, rotate, and store your jars so they're always ready.

I'll also share the things you won't find in a government brochure — like why I use a grape leaf in my pickle jars for crunch, or how I prep jars by the dozen on our wood stove when the power goes out.

A Note from My Heart to Yours

Friend, don't let this world make you fearful. Let it make you *faithful*. Preparing meals in jars isn't about panic. It's about peace. It's about stewardship, wisdom, and caring well for the ones God has placed under your roof.

Start with one jar. Then another. Build slowly, faithfully. And remember — you don't have to do it all at once. Even a small stockpile can be a mighty blessing in the right moment.

So grab your jars, tie on your apron, and let's fill those shelves. We've got work to do — and it's good, honest, holy work.

CHAPTER 1: THE BASICS OF MEALS IN A JAR

There's something deeply satisfying about a pantry shelf lined with jars of complete meals — like standing in the fruit of your labor, knowing your family is covered come what may. But getting those jars to last not just for months, but decades, takes more than good intentions. It takes knowledge, practice, and a few tricks learned from experience.

Understanding the Concept: Meals That Last and Nourish

A meal in a jar is more than just a recipe—it's a carefully layered system designed for shelf-stability, flavor, and convenience. Each ingredient has a role to play and a place in the jar. Layering isn't just about aesthetics (though a jar of rainbow-layered soup mix sure is pretty). It's about keeping ingredients separate when needed, preserving texture, and preventing spoilage.

For example, I always put powdered dairy or bouillon in a sealed mini bag inside the jar. Why? Because if those fine powders settle and absorb moisture, they can clump or spoil faster. Denser items like pasta or beans go at the bottom to keep the jar stable, while lightweight freeze-dried veggies and seasonings go on top.

Think of it like building a house — the foundation matters. The way you layer ingredients directly affects how long that "house" stands tall and safe.

Shelf-Life Explained: Making Meals That Last 25 Years

The key to long-term preservation lies in three enemies: **moisture, oxygen, and contamination**. You eliminate those, and you've got a fighting chance at 25-year shelf life.

Here's how we do it:

- **Dehydrated and freeze-dried ingredients** are the backbone. Freeze-dried meat and veggies, dehydrated grains, and powdered dairy all store well when fully dry and sealed properly.
- **Vacuum sealing** removes air and slows down oxidation.
- **Oxygen absorbers** mop up any lingering O — essential for avoiding mold and spoilage.
- **Desiccant packs** (for some mixes) absorb stray moisture, especially in humid climates.

I'll be honest — when I first started, I reused old jars and didn't always check my seals. I lost an entire batch of chili mac that way. Now, I test every jar seal with a gentle tug and a check for lid flex. And I only store jars in a cool, dark space — like our root cellar — never in the kitchen cabinets above the stove.

If you follow the process faithfully, meals can last **10 to 25 years**, and still taste fresh when opened. I've opened jars of oatmeal mix from 2010 that smelled as sweet as the day I packed them.

Safety Considerations: Keeping Your Family Healthy

Now let's talk about safety — because all the shelf life in the world isn't worth much if the food inside isn't safe to eat.

The biggest risk with improperly stored meals is **botulism**, a rare but deadly foodborne illness. Thankfully, dry storage (under 10% moisture) virtually eliminates that risk — which is why every ingredient going into your jars must be bone dry. No exceptions.

Before eating any meal, do a simple three-step inspection:

1. **Look** — Is the jar intact? No cracks, no rust, no powder clumping?
2. **Smell** — Does it smell fresh? Off-odors are your first red flag.
3. **Listen** — When you open the jar, did the lid "pop"? That sound means the vacuum held.

If anything seems wrong, toss it — no regrets. A bad jar isn't worth a trip to the ER.

Best Practices for Monitoring and Rotation

Even shelf-stable meals need attention from time to time. Here's what I do:

- **Label every jar** with the date and contents. I use masking tape and a permanent marker — simple, but effective.

- **Rotate** your oldest meals to the front, and make it a point to eat one jar a week. That way, you're always testing your stock and refreshing your rotation.
- **Inspect** your pantry every season — especially in the spring and fall when temperature swings can wreak havoc.

I keep a notebook right by my pantry door with a simple grid: date, meal, jar count, any notes. It's old-school, but it keeps me organized when life gets busy.

CHAPTER 2: ESSENTIAL EQUIPMENT AND SUPPLIES

You don't need a fancy setup or a room full of gadgets to make meals in a jar — but having the *right* tools makes the work faster, safer, and a whole lot more enjoyable. In this chapter, I'll walk you through the must-haves, the nice-to-haves, and the downright game-changers that have earned their place in my kitchen.

Types of Jars and Containers: Know Your Vessels

Let's start with the most important piece — the container that holds it all together.

- **Mason Jars**: These are my go-to for most meals. Wide-mouth quart jars are ideal for dinners and soups, while pints work great for breakfasts or single-serve options. Stick with Ball, Kerr, or older Atlas jars — they hold up best over time. Avoid cheap knockoffs from big box stores — I've had too many crack in storage.
- **Mylar Bags**: Great for bulk meals and when you're short on space. Mylar seals tighter and is more puncture-resistant than plastic, especially when paired with oxygen absorbers. I use these when I'm making 10+ servings of something like chili or mac & cheese for our church's disaster relief pantry.
- **Food-Grade Plastic Buckets with Gamma Lids**: Ideal for storing large batches of dry goods like flour, rice, or beans. I keep mine in the pantry for easy scoop-and-fill when I'm assembling new jars.

Space-Saving Tip: I use stackable plastic crates in our root cellar to organize jars by category — breakfasts, soups, stews, and so on. Label each crate clearly and you'll thank yourself later.

Lids and Seals: Securing the Seal

It's not just the jar that matters — the lid is your first line of defense against spoilage.

- **Metal Canning Lids**: Standard Ball or Kerr flat lids work beautifully, especially if vacuum-sealed. Just be sure to use a new lid for long-term storage — reusing them can compromise the seal.
- **Tattler Reusable Lids**: A good option for sustainable storage, though they can be finicky. Make sure you get that "click" when the jar cools and that the rubber ring is properly seated.
- **Screw Bands**: You don't need to leave these on for vacuum-sealed dry meals, but I keep them on loosely for stacking stability.

Faulty Seal Detection Tip: If a lid ever "gives" when you press it, or makes a dull "thunk" instead of a crisp pop, it didn't seal right — don't risk it. Repackage and reseal.

Vacuum Sealers and Oxygen Absorbers: The Dynamic Duo

I call these two the secret weapons of long-term food storage.

- **Vacuum Sealers**: I use a FoodSaver with a jar sealer attachment. It sucks the air out of dry jars like a champ. Just be sure the rim is clean and the lid flat. (Pro tip: if your seal isn't holding, warm the lid a few seconds with a hairdryer before sealing — works wonders.)
- **Oxygen Absorbers (OAs)**: You want 300cc to 500cc absorbers for quart jars, depending on contents. Always store extras in a mason jar with a tight lid or vacuum-sealed bag. If they're soft and pliable, they're still active. Hard as a rock? Toss 'em.

These two tools alone can extend your meals' shelf life from a few years to a few *decades*. I never pack a meal without them.

Tools for Filling and Sealing: The Little Things That Make Life Easier

You'll save time and sanity with these simple tools:

- **Wide-Mouth Funnels**: Essential for keeping things tidy when pouring in powders, grains, or beans. Stainless steel is best.
- **Scoops & Measuring Cups**: I keep a dedicated set just for dry storage meals so I'm not washing mid-process.
- **Desiccant Packs**: Not always necessary, but I use them in humid months or when storing sugar, powdered cheese, or flour-heavy mixes.

- **Label Maker or Permanent Marker**: A labeled jar is a safe jar. Don't trust your memory, especially when your taco soup looks suspiciously like minestrone.
- **Vacuum Sealer Jar Attachment**: Worth every penny. I've used mine weekly for the last five years.

Meal prep days go smoother when your tools are organized and ready. I keep a "jar day kit" in a tote bin with everything I need, so when I've got a quiet afternoon or the woodstove's humming along, I can knock out 8–10 jars without missing a beat.

CHAPTER 3: CHOOSING AND PREPARING INGREDIENTS

If the jar is your vessel and the seal your security, then the ingredients inside are the soul of the meal. This chapter is all about choosing the right building blocks — not just for safety and storage, but for taste, nutrition, and satisfaction. Because when the lights go out or money gets tight, you're going to want meals that warm more than just the belly.

Selecting Shelf-Stable Foods: The Backbone of Your Pantry

Here are the staples I rely on year after year, the workhorses of my jars:

- **Grains**: White rice, quick oats, quinoa, pasta, barley, and wheat berries. Stick to varieties with low oil content — brown rice goes rancid faster.
- **Legumes**: Lentils, split peas, black beans, navy beans. Pre-cooked and dehydrated beans save time and fuel.
- **Powdered Eggs & Dairy**: I buy farm-fresh eggs and dry them myself in small batches, but for long-term storage I use high-quality powdered eggs, butter powder, and milk. These come from suppliers like Augason Farms and Thrive Life.
- **Freeze-Dried Meats & Veggies**: Shelf-stable for 20–25 years. Think ground beef, sausage crumbles, chicken chunks, mushrooms, carrots, bell peppers, spinach, even cheese.
- **Seasonings & Add-ins**: Bouillon, powdered tomato, onion, garlic, spices, and herbs. These are what turn rice and beans into a meal.

Best Bulk Sources: I buy in bulk from Azure Standard, Honeyville, Emergency Essentials, and our local co-op. I also barter with neighbors for eggs and produce to dehydrate at home.

Freeze-Dried vs. Dehydrated: Know the Difference

This one's important.

- **Freeze-Dried** foods are crisp, retain their shape, and rehydrate beautifully. Best for meats, delicate veggies, dairy, and fruits. They cost more, but last 25+ years.
- **Dehydrated** foods are shriveled, denser, and often cheaper. They're great for dense items like onions, carrots, potatoes, and some fruits. Shelf life is closer to 5–10 years, but still valuable.

When to Use What:

- Use freeze-dried meat for meals where texture matters (like stew or pasta).
- Use dehydrated veggies in soups, casseroles, or blended into powders.
- I often mix both to save money — freeze-dried for the core, dehydrated for fillers.

Nutritional Considerations: Fuel for the Long Haul

This isn't about counting calories — it's about ensuring your family has **energy, protein, and balance** when they need it most.

- **Calorie-dense grains** like oats and pasta provide energy.
- **Protein-rich legumes** and meats build strength.
- **Healthy fats** (powdered butter, nuts, seeds) offer satiety and nourishment.

Adjusting for Needs:

- Kids need gentler seasoning and quick-to-chew meals.
- Elderly folks may need lower sodium and softer textures.
- Allergies? Keep separate prep days and label every jar with potential allergens.

I always keep a few jars on hand with no dairy, no gluten, and no meat — just in case we need to share with someone whose needs differ.

Prepping Ingredients: Do It Right the First Time

This is where you can make or break your shelf life.

- **Slicing & Drying**: Thin, uniform slices dry faster and more evenly. I use a mandolin and my Excalibur dehydrator for most items.
- **Blending**: Powders (like onion or tomato) store best when ultra-fine. A high-speed blender helps make these silky smooth.
- **Storing Ingredients**: Before assembly, I store bulk items in mason jars or 5-gallon buckets with oxygen absorbers. Don't open these containers until jar assembly day.

Pro Tip: Let your dried foods "condition" for 24 hours in a loose-lid container after drying — it evens out moisture and prevents spoilage in storage.

Choosing and preparing your ingredients is where the real power begins. This is you saying: *I know what's in our food. I made it myself. And I'm ready for whatever comes next.*

CHAPTER 4: STEP-BY-STEP JAR MEAL PREPARATION

This is the part where it all comes together — the jars, the tools, and the carefully chosen ingredients. It might seem simple, but proper preparation is what separates a dependable 25-year meal from a failed experiment. I've had both, and I promise, it pays to get this part right the first time.

Filling and Layering Techniques: The Order Matters

Layering is about more than looks — it's about food safety, flavor, and function. Here's my typical order:

1. Dense ingredients first — beans, rice, pasta.
2. Veggies next — freeze-dried carrots, corn, onions.
3. Seasonings and bouillon — in a mini zip bag or nested cupcake liner to prevent them from dispersing.
4. Powders and dairy — always on top, sealed separately if possible.

Avoid These Common Mistakes:

- Don't put powder at the bottom — it'll compact and might trap moisture.
- Don't mix bouillon or dairy directly into other ingredients unless vacuum-sealing thoroughly.
- Always inspect for sharp edges — freeze-dried meat can puncture Mylar if you're not careful.

I gently tap the jar on a towel-lined surface to settle ingredients, but never pack them tightly. Airflow and even moisture distribution during rehydration matter.

Sealing for Maximum Shelf Life: Lock It Down

There are three primary sealing methods:

1. **Vacuum Sealing (with Jar Attachment)**: Best for mason jars. Sucks out air, creates a seal with the lid.
2. **Heat Sealing (for Mylar)**: Use an impulse sealer or a flat iron on high heat. Run a double seal for extra safety.
3. **Oxygen Absorbers**: Drop into the jar *last* before sealing. I use 300–500cc for quarts, 100–200cc for pints.

Tips to Avoid Mistakes:

- Always inspect jar rims — even a tiny chip can ruin the seal.
- Wipe the rim with a dry cloth before placing the lid.
- Press down gently on the lid while vacuum sealing to ensure contact.
- For Mylar, let the O absorber work 30–60 seconds before sealing fully.

Labeling and Storage Tips: Don't Skip This!

I've made the mistake of thinking "I'll remember what's in this jar." I didn't. Each jar label should include:

- Meal name (e.g., "Creamy Chicken Alfredo")
- Ingredients (brief, for allergy awareness)
- Date sealed
- Cooking instructions (e.g., "Add 3 cups boiling water. Let sit 15 min.")

Storage Conditions:

- Cool: below 70°F is ideal.
- Dark: UV light degrades nutrients.
- Dry: humidity is a shelf-life killer.

I store mine in our basement root cellar on metal shelves. In summer, I run a dehumidifier nearby. In winter, a wool blanket keeps the shelf dark and insulated.

Testing and Rotating Your Stock: Use What You Store

Even with a 25-year shelf life, you should be *using* your meals regularly. Not just for freshness, but for practice.

Rotation Tips:

- Eat your oldest meals first — I write "Eat by" dates in Sharpie on the lids.

- Schedule a "jar night" once a week. Let the family choose a jar meal for supper.
- Keep a taste-test notebook. If something needs more salt or a spice tweak, write it down for next batch day.

Safe Taste Testing:

- Check for seal integrity before opening.
- Look, smell, inspect before rehydrating.
- If anything seems off, trust your instincts and toss it.

This chapter turns ingredients into preparedness. It's the hands-on, heart-at-peace part of the process — stacking a meal with purpose, sealing it tight, and placing it on the shelf like a small act of providence.

CHAPTER 5: BREAKFASTS

Hearty Starts for Uncertain Days

On our homestead, breakfast has always been more than just a meal. It's a rhythm setter. It fuels the chores, the homeschooling, the woodcutting, and everything in between. And when the grid goes down or time is tight, having wholesome, ready-to-go breakfasts in jars isn't just convenient — it's a lifeline.

These meals are tried and true, made with shelf-stable ingredients that last for years. They're simple to prepare, family-friendly, and hearty enough to carry you well into the morning. I've packed every one of these for emergencies and lazy Sundays alike.

Instant Oatmeal with Fruit and Nuts

Per serving jar:

- ½ cup quick oats
- 2 Tbsp chopped dried apples
- 1 Tbsp raisins
- 1 Tbsp chopped walnuts
- 2 Tbsp powdered milk
- ½ tsp cinnamon
- Pinch of salt
- 1 tsp brown sugar or ½ tsp maple powder (optional)

To Make: Add ¾ cup boiling water. Stir, cover, and let sit 5–10 minutes. Stir again and enjoy.

Blueberry Pancake Mix

Per serving jar (makes 2–3 pancakes):

- ½ cup all-purpose flour
- 1 tsp baking powder
- ¼ tsp salt
- 1 tsp sugar
- 1 Tbsp powdered egg
- 2 Tbsp powdered milk or buttermilk
- 2 Tbsp freeze-dried blueberries

To Make: Add about ⅓ cup water gradually while stirring until you get a thick batter. Cook on a greased skillet over medium heat until golden on both sides.

Cinnamon Raisin Breakfast Rice Pudding

Per serving jar:

- ½ cup instant white rice
- 2 Tbsp powdered milk
- 1 Tbsp sugar
- 1 Tbsp raisins
- ½ tsp cinnamon
- Pinch of salt

To Make: Add ¾ to 1 cup boiling water. Stir well, cover, and let sit 10–15 minutes. Reheat if desired, or eat warm as-is.

Scrambled Eggs with Bacon Bits

Per serving jar:

- 2 Tbsp powdered eggs
- 1 Tbsp freeze-dried cheddar
- 1 Tbsp real bacon bits
- Pinch of pepper

To Make: Mix with ¼ cup cold water. Let sit 1 minute. Scramble in a hot, greased skillet over medium heat, stirring constantly until fully cooked.

Apple Cinnamon Granola Parfait

Per serving jar:

- ½ cup granola
- 2 Tbsp freeze-dried apple slices, crumbled

- 2 Tbsp powdered yogurt or milk
- ¼ tsp cinnamon

To Make: Add ¼ cup warm water and stir. Let sit 5–10 minutes to soften. Eat as-is or refrigerate.

Cheesy Grits and Sausage

Per serving jar:

- ½ cup instant grits
- 2 Tbsp powdered cheddar
- 2 Tbsp freeze-dried sausage crumbles
- ¼ tsp onion powder
- ⅛ tsp garlic powder

To Make: Add 1 cup boiling water, stir, cover, and let sit 5–10 minutes. Stir before eating.

Strawberry Cream Wheat

Per serving jar:

- ½ cup instant cream of wheat
- 2 Tbsp powdered strawberries
- 2 Tbsp powdered milk
- 1 tsp sugar
- Pinch of salt

To Make: Add ¾ cup boiling water, stir well, and let sit 5 minutes. Stir again before eating.

Hash Browns and Veggie Skillet

Per serving jar:

- ½ cup dehydrated shredded potatoes
- 1 Tbsp freeze-dried peppers
- 1 Tbsp freeze-dried onions
- 1 Tbsp freeze-dried mushrooms or bacon bits (optional)

To Make: Add just enough boiling water to cover. Let sit 10–15 minutes. Drain thoroughly, then fry in 1 Tbsp oil until browned and crispy.

Peanut Butter Banana Oatmeal

Per serving jar:

- ½ cup quick oats
- 1 Tbsp powdered peanut butter
- 1 Tbsp banana chips, crushed
- ¼ tsp nutmeg
- Pinch of salt

To Make: Add ¾ cup boiling water, stir well, cover, and wait 5–7 minutes. Stir again before serving.

French Toast Casserole

Per serving jar:

- ½ cup cubed dried bread
- 1 Tbsp powdered egg
- 2 Tbsp powdered milk
- ½ tsp cinnamon
- ¼ tsp vanilla powder
- 1 tsp sugar

To Make: Add ½ cup hot water, stir gently to moisten all pieces. Let sit 10 minutes, then bake in oven-safe dish or fry gently in skillet until golden.

Pumpkin Spice Overnight Oats

Per serving jar:

- ½ cup rolled oats
- 1 Tbsp pumpkin powder
- 2 Tbsp powdered milk
- ½ tsp cinnamon
- ¼ tsp nutmeg
- 1 tsp brown sugar

To Make: Add ½ cup water, stir, and refrigerate or let sit in cool place overnight. Stir before serving.

Maple Pecan Quinoa Bowl

Per serving jar:

- ½ cup quinoa flakes
- 1 Tbsp maple sugar
- 2 Tbsp powdered milk
- 1 Tbsp chopped pecans

To Make: Add ¾ cup boiling water, stir, cover, and let sit 10 minutes. Stir again and enjoy warm.

These breakfasts have filled my family's bellies on stormy mornings, during travel, and even on quiet days at home when I needed a break from cooking. A pantry full of these jars means you're always one step ahead — with nourishment, peace of mind, and the assurance that no matter what the day holds, you've started it right.

More Breakfast Recipes.

Recipe Name	Ingredients (per jar)	To Make
Almond Apricot Couscous	½ cup instant couscous, 2 Tbsp chopped dried apricots, 2 Tbsp sliced almonds, 1 Tbsp milk powder, pinch of cardamom	Add ¾ cup boiling water. Stir, cover tightly, and let sit 5–7 minutes. Fluff with fork and serve warm.
Breakfast Barley with Berries	½ cup pearl barley flakes, 2 Tbsp freeze-dried raspberries, 1 Tbsp powdered honey, 2 Tbsp milk powder	Add ¾ cup hot water. Stir well, cover, and let sit 10–15 minutes. Stir again before serving.
Coconut Mango Chia Porridge	2 Tbsp chia seeds, 2 Tbsp powdered coconut milk, 2 Tbsp dried mango bits, 1 Tbsp oat flour, pinch of ginger	Add ¾ cup hot water, stir well. Let sit 10–15 minutes or refrigerate overnight for cold porridge. Stir before eating.
Cheddar Bacon Biscuit Mix	¾ cup biscuit mix (with flour, baking powder, salt), 1 Tbsp powdered egg, 2 Tbsp powdered cheddar, 2 Tbsp bacon crumbles	Mix with ⅓ cup water to form soft dough. Drop spoonfuls onto hot skillet or baking sheet. Cook until golden, 10–12 mins.
Spiced Carrot Breakfast Bowl	½ cup instant oats, 2 Tbsp powdered carrots, ½ tsp cinnamon, ¼ tsp ginger, 1 Tbsp raisins, 2 Tbsp milk powder	Add ¾ cup boiling water, stir well, cover, and let sit 5–10 minutes. Stir again and serve warm.
Savory Breakfast Lentils	¼ cup quick-cook red lentils, 1 tsp freeze-dried onion, 1 tsp tomato powder, ¼ tsp cumin, ¼ tsp garlic powder	Add ¾ cup boiling water. Cover and let sit 10 minutes. Stir and serve, or fry in a skillet with oil for a crispy version.
Peach Cobbler Oatmeal	½ cup rolled oats, 2 Tbsp chopped dried peaches, ¼ tsp cinnamon, 1 Tbsp brown sugar, 2 Tbsp milk powder, 1 Tbsp crumbled vanilla cookie bits	Add ¾ cup hot water. Stir well, cover, and let sit 5–10 minutes. Stir again before eating.
Cranberry Orange Rice Bowl	½ cup instant rice, 2 Tbsp dried cranberries, ½ tsp orange zest powder, 1 Tbsp milk powder, 1 Tbsp honey powder	Add ¾ cup boiling water. Stir well, cover, and let sit 10 minutes. Fluff and serve.
Tomato Basil Egg Scramble Mix	2 Tbsp powdered eggs, 1 Tbsp freeze-dried tomato, ¼ tsp basil, ⅛ tsp garlic powder, 1 Tbsp cheddar powder	Mix with ¼ cup water until smooth. Scramble in greased skillet over medium heat until firm and fluffy.

Breakfast Stuffing Hash	½ cup dried bread cubes, 2 Tbsp freeze-dried sausage, 1 tsp celery flakes, ¼ tsp onion powder, ⅛ tsp sage	Add ½ cup hot broth or water. Let soak 10 minutes. Pan-fry with a little oil until golden and crispy.
Chocolate Banana Porridge	¼ cup oat bran, 2 Tbsp crushed banana chips, 1 Tbsp cocoa powder, 2 Tbsp milk powder, pinch of cinnamon	Add ¾ cup boiling water. Stir thoroughly. Let sit 5 minutes. Stir again and serve warm.
Savory Polenta with Herbs	½ cup instant polenta, 2 Tbsp cheese powder, ½ tsp chive flakes, ¼ tsp onion powder, pinch of salt	Add 1 cup boiling water, stir constantly until thick. Let sit 3–5 minutes, or simmer for smoother texture.

CHAPTER 6: LUNCHES

Midday Fuel for Real Life

Midday meals should be simple but satisfying — especially when you're deep into chores, running kids between homeschool lessons, or managing a crisis. These jarred lunches were born out of necessity, but they've become staples around here. They're quick to prepare, packed with nourishment, and they hold up just as well on a quiet afternoon as they do in an emergency.

You'll notice a theme in many of these recipes: hearty grains, good protein, and plenty of vegetables. Whether you're filling bellies on the go or hunkering down in a storm, these meals are designed to bring comfort and strength when you need it most.

Hearty Minestrone Soup

Per jar (1 generous serving):

- ¼ cup small pasta (elbow or ditalini)
- 2 Tbsp dehydrated red or white beans (pre-cooked or quick-soak type)
- 1 Tbsp tomato powder
- 2 Tbsp freeze-dried mixed vegetables (carrot, green bean, zucchini)
- ¼ tsp dried basil
- ¼ tsp oregano
- ⅛ tsp garlic powder
- Pinch of black pepper

To Make: Add 1½ cups boiling water. Stir, cover, and let sit 15–20 minutes. For quicker prep, simmer on stovetop 10 minutes until pasta is tender.

Creamy Potato and Bacon Chowder

Per jar:

- ½ cup potato flakes
- 2 Tbsp powdered milk
- 1 Tbsp cheese powder
- 1 Tbsp freeze-dried onion
- 1 Tbsp real bacon bits
- ¼ tsp parsley (optional)
- Pinch of salt and pepper

To Make: Add 1 cup boiling water, stir well, cover, and let sit 10–12 minutes. Stir before eating.

Vegetable and Rice Pilaf

Per jar:

- ½ cup instant white rice
- 1 Tbsp freeze-dried carrot
- 1 Tbsp freeze-dried peas
- 1 Tbsp freeze-dried bell pepper
- 1 tsp freeze-dried onion
- ¼ tsp thyme
- ¼ tsp garlic powder
- Pinch of salt

To Make: Add 1 cup boiling water, stir, cover, and let sit 10 minutes. Fluff with fork before serving.

Black Bean and Corn Soup

Per jar:

- 2 Tbsp dehydrated black beans
- 2 Tbsp freeze-dried corn
- 1 Tbsp tomato powder
- 1 tsp freeze-dried onion
- ¼ tsp cumin
- ⅛ tsp chili powder
- Pinch of lime powder or citric acid

To Make: Add 1½ cups boiling water. Stir and let sit 20–25 minutes, or simmer gently until beans are soft.

Chicken Salad (Just Add Water)

Per jar:

- ¼ cup freeze-dried chicken
- 1 Tbsp freeze-dried celery
- 1 tsp freeze-dried onion
- ¼ tsp garlic powder
- Pinch of salt and pepper

To Make: Add 2–3 Tbsp cool water and stir until moistened. Let sit 10 minutes. Best served with added mayo or oil if available, on crackers or flatbread.

Classic Tomato Basil Soup

Per jar:

- 2 Tbsp tomato powder
- 2 Tbsp powdered milk
- ½ tsp dried basil
- ¼ tsp onion powder
- ⅛ tsp garlic powder
- ½ tsp sugar
- Pinch of salt

To Make: Add 1 cup boiling water, whisk until smooth, and let sit covered for 5 minutes. Stir again and serve hot.

Mac & Cheese with Broccoli

Per jar:

- ½ cup elbow pasta
- 2 Tbsp cheese powder
- 1 Tbsp powdered milk
- 1 Tbsp freeze-dried broccoli florets, crumbled
- Pinch of onion powder

To Make: Add enough boiling water to cover pasta (about 1¼ cups). Stir, cover, and let sit 10–12 minutes, or simmer on stovetop for 8–10 minutes. Stir again until creamy.

Curried Lentil Soup

Per jar:

- ¼ cup red lentils

- 1 Tbsp dehydrated carrot
- 1 tsp dehydrated onion
- ½ tsp curry powder
- ¼ tsp garlic powder
- Pinch of ginger
- ½ tsp salt

To Make: Add 1½ cups boiling water, stir, and let sit 20 minutes, or simmer 15 minutes until lentils are soft.

Beef & Barley Stew

Per jar:

- 2 Tbsp freeze-dried beef
- 2 Tbsp barley
- 1 Tbsp freeze-dried carrots
- 1 Tbsp freeze-dried peas
- 1 tsp freeze-dried onion
- ½ tsp garlic powder
- ½ tsp beef bouillon powder
- Pinch of pepper

To Make: Add 1½ cups boiling water, stir, cover, and let sit 20–25 minutes, or simmer gently until barley is tender.

Taco Soup with Beans and Corn

Per jar:

- 1 Tbsp dehydrated kidney beans
- 1 Tbsp black beans
- 2 Tbsp freeze-dried corn
- 1 Tbsp tomato powder
- 1 tsp freeze-dried onion
- ¼ tsp cumin
- ¼ tsp chili powder
- 1 Tbsp cheese powder (optional)
- Pinch of salt

To Make: Add 1½ cups boiling water. Stir, cover, and let sit 20–25 minutes, or simmer gently. Serve with crackers, chips, or cornbread if available.

BONUS: Creamy Mushroom Barley Soup

Per jar:

- 1 Tbsp freeze-dried mushrooms
- 2 Tbsp barley
- 1 tsp freeze-dried onion
- ½ tsp thyme
- 1 Tbsp powdered cream (or whole milk powder)
- Salt and pepper to taste

To Make: Add 1¼ cups boiling water. Stir, cover, and let sit 15–20 minutes, or simmer until barley is soft.

BONUS: Sweet and Sour Cabbage Stew

Per jar:

- ¼ cup dehydrated cabbage
- 1 Tbsp tomato powder
- 1 tsp freeze-dried onion
- 1 tsp raisins
- ¼ tsp vinegar powder (or ⅛ tsp citric acid)
- 1 tsp sugar
- Pinch of salt and pepper

To Make: Add 1½ cups boiling water. Stir, simmer gently 10–15 minutes until cabbage is tender.

Lunch doesn't have to be complicated to be good. With these jars on your shelf, you'll always have something hearty, hot, and homemade to keep you going — even when the world outside feels a little upside down.

More Lunch Recipes.

Recipe Name	Ingredients (per jar)	To Make
Tuna Pasta Salad (Shelf-Stable)	½ cup freeze-dried tuna, ½ cup pasta shells, 1 tsp celery flakes, 1 tsp onion flakes, ¼ tsp dill, 1 Tbsp mayo powder	Add ⅓–½ cup cool water to moisten. Stir and let sit 10 minutes. Serve chilled or at room temp. Optional: Add 1 tsp oil or vinegar if available.
Creamy Chickpea Curry Bowl	¼ cup instant chickpeas, 2 Tbsp coconut milk powder, ½ tsp curry powder, 1 tsp onion flakes, 1 tsp tomato powder	Add 1 cup boiling water. Stir, cover, and let sit 15–20 minutes or simmer gently until chickpeas soften. Stir before serving.
Cheesy Polenta with Veggies	½ cup instant polenta, 2 Tbsp cheese powder, 1 Tbsp milk powder, 1 Tbsp freeze-dried zucchini, 1 Tbsp freeze-dried carrots	Add 1 cup boiling water. Stir constantly until thickened. Let sit 5–7 minutes, stir again, and serve warm.

Recipe	Ingredients	Instructions
Italian Sausage & Orzo Soup	2 Tbsp freeze-dried sausage, ¼ cup orzo pasta, 1 Tbsp tomato powder, ¼ tsp garlic powder, ¼ tsp dried basil, 1 tsp onion flakes	Add 1½ cups boiling water. Stir, cover, and let sit 10–15 minutes or simmer until pasta is tender.
Stuffed Pepper Soup Starter	½ cup instant rice, 1 Tbsp tomato powder, 2 Tbsp freeze-dried ground beef, 1 Tbsp bell pepper flakes, 1 tsp onion flakes, ¼ tsp Italian herb blend	Add 1½ cups boiling water. Stir, cover, and let sit 15 minutes or simmer gently. Stir again before serving.
Thai Peanut Noodle Bowl	½ cup instant rice noodles, 2 Tbsp powdered peanut butter, ½ tsp soy sauce powder, ⅛ tsp ginger powder, ⅛ tsp lime powder, 1 tsp green onion flakes	Add 1 cup boiling water. Stir until noodles are soft and sauce is thickened, about 10 minutes. Add hot sauce if desired.
Split Pea Soup with Ham Flavor	¼ cup split peas, 1 tsp ham broth powder, 1 tsp onion flakes, 1 tsp carrot flakes, 1 tsp celery flakes, pinch of thyme	Add 1½ cups boiling water. Stir, cover, and simmer 20–25 minutes until peas are soft. Stir occasionally.
Zesty Tomato Tortellini Soup	½ cup dried cheese tortellini, 1 Tbsp tomato powder, ¼ tsp garlic powder, ¼ tsp basil, 1 tsp onion flakes, pinch of red pepper flakes	Add 1½ cups boiling water. Cover and let sit 10–12 minutes or simmer gently until tortellini are soft. Stir before serving.
Jambalaya Rice Bowl	½ cup instant rice, 2 Tbsp freeze-dried chicken or sausage, 1 Tbsp bell pepper flakes, 1 tsp onion flakes, 1 Tbsp tomato powder, ½ tsp Cajun seasoning	Add 1¼ cups boiling water. Stir, cover, and let sit 10–15 minutes or simmer gently. Stir before serving.
Southwest Quinoa Chili	¼ cup quinoa flakes, 2 Tbsp black beans, 1 Tbsp freeze-dried corn, 1 Tbsp tomato powder, ½ tsp cumin, ½ tsp chili powder	Add 1½ cups boiling water. Stir, cover, and let sit 15 minutes or simmer gently until thick. Stir before eating.
Creamy Tuna & Corn Chowder	¼ cup freeze-dried tuna, 2 Tbsp freeze-dried corn, ¼ cup potato flakes, 2 Tbsp milk powder, 1 tsp onion flakes, ¼ tsp dill	Add 1¼ cups boiling water. Stir well, cover, and let sit 10–12 minutes. Stir again before serving.
Lemon Herb Couscous Bowl	½ cup instant couscous, 2 Tbsp freeze-dried chicken, ½ tsp lemon zest powder, ¼ tsp parsley, ¼ tsp garlic powder, 1 Tbsp freeze-dried peas	Add ¾ cup boiling water. Stir, cover, and let sit 5 minutes. Fluff with fork before serving.
Broccoli Cheddar Soup Starter	2 Tbsp cheese powder, 2 Tbsp milk powder, 2 Tbsp freeze-dried broccoli, 1 tsp onion flakes, ¼ cup potato flakes	Add 1¼ cups boiling water. Stir until smooth. Cover and let sit 10 minutes or simmer gently for creamier texture.

CHAPTER 7: DINNERS

Dinner is sacred in our home. It's when we sit down, give thanks, and reconnect after the work of the day. And in uncertain times, having complete, hearty suppers ready to go isn't just practical — it's a way of keeping hope alive.

These jarred meals aren't just "good enough for emergencies." They're real food. Suppers you'd proudly serve even if nothing was wrong. Each recipe is designed for ease of use, maximum shelf life, and a deep, satisfying flavor that warms more than just the stomach.

Classic Beef Stroganoff

Per jar:

- ¼ cup freeze-dried ground beef
- ½ cup egg noodles
- 1 Tbsp sour cream powder
- 1 tsp freeze-dried onion
- 1 Tbsp freeze-dried mushroom
- ¼ tsp garlic powder
- ½ tsp beef bouillon granules
- Pinch of black pepper

To Make: Add 1½ cups boiling water. Stir, cover, and let sit 15 minutes or simmer 10 minutes. Stir until creamy.

Chicken and Dumplings

Per jar (base + topping):
Stew base:

- ¼ cup freeze-dried chicken
- 1 Tbsp freeze-dried carrot
- 1 Tbsp freeze-dried celery
- 1 tsp freeze-dried onion
- 1 tsp herb blend (thyme, sage)
- 1 Tbsp milk powder
- ¼ tsp salt

Dumpling mix:

- ¼ cup biscuit mix
- 1 Tbsp powdered milk

To Make: Rehydrate stew with 1 cup boiling water. Simmer 5 minutes. Mix dumpling topping with 2 Tbsp water to form dough. Drop by spoonfuls into simmering base, cover, and cook 10–15 minutes until dumplings puff up.

Chili Mac and Cheese

Per jar:

- ½ cup elbow pasta
- 2 Tbsp freeze-dried beef or sausage
- 1 Tbsp tomato powder
- 1 Tbsp cheese powder
- 1 Tbsp pre-cooked black or kidney beans
- ¼ tsp chili powder
- ¼ tsp cumin
- ⅛ tsp garlic powder

To Make: Add 1½ cups boiling water, stir, cover, and let sit 12–15 minutes, or simmer gently. Stir again before serving.

Chicken and Vegetable Curry

Per jar:

- ¼ cup freeze-dried chicken
- 2 Tbsp freeze-dried peas
- 2 Tbsp freeze-dried carrots
- 1 Tbsp coconut milk powder

- ¼ tsp curry powder
- ½ cup instant white rice
- ¼ tsp salt

To Make: Add 1½ cups boiling water. Stir, cover, and let sit 15 minutes or simmer gently. Fluff before serving.

Italian Pasta Primavera

Per jar:

- ½ cup small pasta (penne or rotini)
- 1 Tbsp freeze-dried zucchini
- 1 Tbsp freeze-dried bell peppers
- 1 Tbsp freeze-dried tomato
- 1 tsp freeze-dried onion
- ¼ tsp garlic powder
- 1 Tbsp Parmesan cheese powder
- ½ tsp Italian herb blend

To Make: Add 1½ cups boiling water. Stir and simmer 10–12 minutes until pasta is tender.

Vegetarian Quinoa Chili

Per jar:

- ¼ cup quinoa
- 2 Tbsp dehydrated black beans
- 1 Tbsp freeze-dried corn
- 1 Tbsp tomato powder
- 1 tsp freeze-dried onion
- ¼ tsp chili powder
- ¼ tsp smoked paprika
- ¼ tsp garlic powder

To Make: Add 1½ cups boiling water. Simmer 15–20 minutes until quinoa is fluffy and beans are soft.

Lentil and Sausage Stew

Per jar:

- ¼ cup brown lentils
- 2 Tbsp freeze-dried sausage crumbles
- 1 Tbsp freeze-dried carrot
- 1 tsp freeze-dried onion

- ¼ tsp garlic powder
- ¼ tsp thyme
- Pinch of pepper

To Make: Add 1½ cups boiling water. Cover and simmer 20 minutes until lentils are tender.

Beef and Mushroom Risotto

Per jar:

- ¼ cup arborio rice
- 2 Tbsp freeze-dried beef
- 1 Tbsp freeze-dried mushrooms
- 1 tsp freeze-dried onion
- 1 Tbsp cream powder
- ¼ tsp garlic powder
- ½ tsp beef bouillon

To Make: Add 1½ cups boiling water. Simmer gently 15–20 minutes, stirring occasionally until creamy.

Creamy Chicken Alfredo

Per jar:

- ½ cup pasta (fettuccine broken into bits or small shells)
- ¼ cup freeze-dried chicken
- 1 Tbsp cream powder
- 1 Tbsp Parmesan cheese powder
- ¼ tsp garlic powder
- Pinch of black pepper

To Make: Add 1½ cups boiling water. Stir, cover, and let sit 12–15 minutes or simmer gently.

Mexican Fiesta Rice

Per jar:

- ½ cup instant white rice
- 1 Tbsp black beans
- 1 Tbsp freeze-dried corn
- 1 Tbsp tomato powder
- 1 tsp freeze-dried onion
- ¼ tsp cumin
- ¼ tsp chili powder

- 1 Tbsp cheese powder (optional)

To Make: Add 1½ cups boiling water. Stir, cover, and let sit 10–12 minutes, or simmer until rice is soft.

Asian Chicken Fried Rice

Per jar:

- ½ cup instant rice
- 2 Tbsp freeze-dried chicken
- 1 Tbsp freeze-dried peas
- 1 Tbsp freeze-dried carrot
- ½ tsp soy sauce powder
- 1 tsp egg powder
- ¼ tsp garlic powder
- 1 tsp freeze-dried green onion

To Make: Add ¾ cup hot water. Let sit 10 minutes, then sauté in 1 tsp oil in a hot skillet until browned.

Sweet Potato & Black Bean Stew

Per jar:

- ¼ cup dehydrated sweet potato
- 2 Tbsp black beans
- 1 tsp freeze-dried onion
- ¼ tsp garlic powder
- ¼ tsp cumin
- Pinch of cinnamon
- Salt to taste

To Make: Add 1½ cups boiling water. Simmer 15–20 minutes or until sweet potatoes are soft.

Southwest Rice and Beans

Per jar:

- ½ cup instant rice
- 2 Tbsp pinto beans
- 1 Tbsp freeze-dried corn
- 1 Tbsp tomato powder
- 1 tsp freeze-dried onion
- ¼ tsp cumin
- ¼ tsp chili powder

- 1 Tbsp cheese powder (optional)

To Make: Add 1½ cups boiling water. Stir, cover, and let sit 12 minutes or simmer gently.

Shepherd's Pie Mix

Per jar:

- ¼ cup mashed potato flakes
- 2 Tbsp freeze-dried beef
- 1 Tbsp freeze-dried corn
- 1 Tbsp freeze-dried carrot
- 1 tsp freeze-dried onion
- 1 Tbsp beef gravy powder

To Make: Rehydrate stew base with 1 cup boiling water. Mix potato flakes separately with ½ cup boiling water, then spread on top before serving.

Spaghetti and Meat Sauce

Per jar:

- ½ cup pasta (broken spaghetti or macaroni)
- ¼ cup freeze-dried ground beef
- 1 Tbsp tomato powder
- 1 tsp freeze-dried onion
- ¼ tsp garlic powder
- ¼ tsp basil
- ¼ tsp oregano

To Make: Add 1½ cups boiling water. Stir, cover, and simmer 10–12 minutes until pasta is soft.

BONUS: Thai Peanut Noodles

Per jar:

- ½ cup rice noodles
- 1 Tbsp powdered peanut butter
- ½ tsp soy sauce powder
- ⅛ tsp chili flakes
- 1 Tbsp freeze-dried mixed vegetables

To Make: Add 1 cup boiling water. Cover and let sit 10 minutes. Stir until creamy. Add hot sauce if you like heat.

BONUS: Rustic Turkey Pot Pie

Filling per jar:

- ¼ cup freeze-dried turkey
- 2 Tbsp freeze-dried mixed vegetables
- 1 Tbsp cream powder
- 1 tsp poultry seasoning

Biscuit topping mix (separate jar):

- ¼ cup biscuit mix
- 1 Tbsp powdered milk

To Make: Rehydrate filling with 1 cup boiling water. Heat in a pan. Mix biscuit topping with 2 Tbsp water. Drop over filling and pan-steam covered for 10 minutes, or bake uncovered at 350°F for 15 minutes.

These dinners represent more than just calories — they're tradition, care, and resilience in a jar. With a pantry full of meals like these, you're not just surviving — you're living well, even when the world says otherwise.

More Dinner Recipes.

Recipe Name	Ingredients (per Jar)	To Make
Stuffed Pepper Rice Bake	½ cup instant rice, 2 Tbsp freeze-dried ground beef, 1 Tbsp bell pepper flakes, 1 Tbsp tomato powder, 1 tsp onion flakes, ¼ tsp garlic powder, ¼ tsp Italian herbs	Add 1½ cups boiling water. Stir, cover, and let sit 15 minutes or simmer gently until rice is tender. Stir before serving.
Salisbury Steak Stew	2 Tbsp freeze-dried beef, 1 tsp onion flakes, 1 tsp mushroom powder, 1 Tbsp gravy powder, ¼ cup potato flakes, ¼ tsp garlic powder, ¼ tsp dried parsley	Add 1½ cups boiling water. Stir well. Simmer 10–15 minutes until thick and hearty. Stir occasionally.
Ratatouille Pasta Skillet	½ cup pasta, 1 Tbsp freeze-dried zucchini, 1 Tbsp tomato powder, 1 tsp onion flakes, 1 tsp bell pepper flakes, 1 tsp eggplant powder, ¼ tsp basil, ¼ tsp garlic powder	Add enough boiling water to cover. Simmer 10–12 minutes until pasta is tender and vegetables rehydrate. Stir and serve.
Bacon Cheeseburger Casserole	½ cup pasta, 2 Tbsp freeze-dried ground beef, 2 Tbsp cheese powder, 1 Tbsp bacon bits, 1 Tbsp tomato powder, 1 tsp onion flakes, ⅛ tsp mustard powder	Add 1¼ cups boiling water. Stir well. Let sit 10 minutes or simmer gently until creamy and thick.
Savory Ham & Lentil Soup	2 Tbsp freeze-dried ham, ¼ cup green lentils, 1 tsp carrot flakes, 1 tsp celery flakes, 1 tsp	Add 1½ cups boiling water. Simmer 15–20 minutes or until lentils are fully tender. Stir occasionally.

	Ingredients	Instructions
	onion flakes, ¼ tsp garlic powder, pinch of thyme	
Cabbage Roll Soup	2 Tbsp freeze-dried ground beef, 2 Tbsp cabbage flakes, 1 Tbsp tomato powder, 1 tsp onion flakes, ¼ tsp garlic powder, 2 Tbsp instant rice, ¼ tsp paprika	Add 1½ cups boiling water. Simmer 15–20 minutes or until rice and cabbage are tender. Stir before serving.
Creamy Chicken & Wild Rice	2 Tbsp freeze-dried chicken, ¼ cup wild rice blend, 1 tsp carrot flakes, 1 tsp celery flakes, 1 tsp onion flakes, 1 Tbsp cream powder, pinch of thyme	Add 1½–2 cups boiling water. Simmer gently 20–25 minutes until rice is tender and broth is creamy.
Tex-Mex Enchilada Bowl	½ cup instant rice, 2 Tbsp black beans, 2 Tbsp freeze-dried chicken, ½ tsp enchilada seasoning, 1 Tbsp tomato powder, 1 tsp onion flakes, 1 Tbsp cheese powder	Add 1½ cups boiling water. Stir, cover, and let sit 10–15 minutes or simmer until thick and hot.
Moroccan Chickpea Tagine	¼ cup chickpeas, 1 Tbsp tomato powder, 1 tsp onion flakes, ¼ tsp garlic powder, 1 Tbsp chopped dried apricots, pinch of cinnamon, ¼ tsp cumin, ¼ tsp turmeric	Add 1½ cups boiling water. Cover and let sit or simmer 15–20 minutes until thick and aromatic. Stir before serving.
Beefy Macaroni Skillet	½ cup macaroni, 2 Tbsp freeze-dried beef, 1 Tbsp tomato powder, 1 tsp onion flakes, ¼ tsp garlic powder, ¼ tsp Italian herb blend, 1 Tbsp cheese powder	Add 1½ cups boiling water. Stir, cover, and let sit 10 minutes or simmer until pasta is soft and cheesy.
Cajun Red Beans & Rice	¼ cup red beans, ½ cup instant rice, 2 Tbsp freeze-dried sausage, 1 tsp bell pepper flakes, 1 tsp onion flakes, ¼ tsp garlic powder, ½ tsp Cajun seasoning	Add 1½ cups boiling water. Stir, cover, and let sit 15 minutes or simmer gently. Stir again before serving.
Creamy Mushroom Stroganoff	½ cup pasta, 1 Tbsp mushroom powder, 1 tsp onion flakes, ¼ tsp garlic powder, 1 Tbsp cream base, ¼ tsp black pepper, pinch of parsley	Add enough boiling water to cover. Stir well. Let sit 10–12 minutes or simmer until creamy and soft.
Sweet & Savory Pineapple Pork	2 Tbsp freeze-dried pork, 1 Tbsp pineapple powder, 1 Tbsp tomato powder, ¼ tsp garlic powder, 1 tsp bell pepper flakes, ¼ tsp soy sauce powder, 1 tsp onion flakes	Add 1½ cups hot water. Stir and simmer gently 15 minutes until meat is tender and sauce is thickened.
German Potato Sausage Bake	½ cup potato flakes, 2 Tbsp freeze-dried sausage, 1 tsp onion flakes, pinch of caraway seed, ¼ tsp garlic powder, ⅛ tsp mustard powder	Add 1¼ cups boiling water. Stir until thickened. Let sit 10 minutes. Optional: crisp in skillet for crusty topping.
Hearty Bison & Veggie Stew	2 Tbsp freeze-dried bison, 1 Tbsp carrot flakes, 1 Tbsp potato flakes, 1 tsp onion flakes, ¼ tsp garlic powder, pinch of rosemary, ½ tsp beef bouillon powder	Add 1½–2 cups boiling water. Simmer gently 20–25 minutes or until meat and vegetables are tender.

CHAPTER 8: SNACKS

Morale Boosters and Energy Lifters in Every Jar

There's no denying it — snacks are essential. Not just to curb hunger between meals, but to lift moods, give energy, and offer a touch of normal when life feels anything but. Whether it's a handful of trail mix during firewood chores, or something crunchy to keep the kids content during a power outage, these snacks have earned their place in our long-term pantry.

What I love about these recipes is that they're packable, nutritious, and most importantly — they taste good. These aren't "just get by" snacks. They're treats we make even when the grid's humming and life is calm.

Trail Mix Jars

Base Mix (per pint jar):

- ¼ cup almonds
- ¼ cup sunflower seeds
- ¼ cup raisins or dried cranberries
- 2 Tbsp mini chocolate chips (omit if storing warm)
- ¼ cup pretzel pieces (optional)

To Store: Vacuum seal with 1 oxygen absorber. Rotate seasonally.
Shelf Life: 6–12 months sealed; up to 18 months if cool, dry, and dark.

Spicy Roasted Chickpeas

Ingredients:

- 1 cup cooked chickpeas (fully dried after boiling)
- 1 tsp olive oil or butter powder
- ½ tsp garlic powder
- ¼ tsp smoked paprika
- ¼ tsp cayenne
- ¼ tsp salt

To Make: Toss chickpeas in oil/spice blend. Dehydrate at 125–135°F for 10–12 hours until completely dry and crisp.
Storage: Mason jars with desiccant.
Shelf Life: 6 months to 1 year.

Dehydrated Fruit Blend

Suggested blend (per quart):

- 1 cup apple slices
- ½ cup banana coins
- ½ cup strawberry halves
- ½ cup mango strips
- ¼ cup blueberries

To Make: Dehydrate fruits separately at 125°F until leathery or crisp. Condition for 5–7 days (shake daily to check moisture). Combine and seal.
Storage: Vacuum seal with oxygen absorber.
Shelf Life: 1 year+ in cool storage.

Honey Granola Clusters

Batch (fills 1–2 quarts):

- 2 cups rolled oats
- ½ cup honey powder + 2 Tbsp water
- ¼ cup shredded coconut
- ½ cup chopped almonds or walnuts
- 1 tsp cinnamon
- Pinch of salt

To Make: Mix ingredients, press into small clusters on dehydrator trays. Dry at 135°F for 10–12 hours until crisp.
Storage: Mylar or vacuum-sealed jars with desiccant.

Cinnamon Sugar Apple Chips

Per batch (2 trays):

- 3 medium apples, thinly sliced

- 1 tsp cinnamon
- 1 Tbsp sugar

To Make: Toss slices in cinnamon-sugar, then dehydrate at 135°F for 10–14 hours until crisp.
Storage: Airtight jars with desiccant.
Shelf Life: 6–12 months sealed.

Garlic & Herb Pretzel Mix

Per batch:

- 2 cups pretzel twists, lightly crushed
- 2 Tbsp butter powder
- 1 tsp garlic powder
- ½ tsp onion powder
- 1 tsp dried parsley

To Make: Toss pretzels in seasoning. Bake at 250°F for 15 minutes. Cool fully, then vacuum seal.
Note: Store cool to prevent oil rancidity.

Cheesy Vegetable Crackers

Per dough batch:

- 1 cup flour
- ½ cup cheese powder
- ¼ cup powdered spinach or carrot
- 2 Tbsp butter powder
- ¼ tsp salt
- ¼ cup water (adjust as needed)

To Make: Roll dough thin, cut into squares. Bake at 350°F for 12–15 minutes. Dehydrate baked crackers at 125°F for 6 hours to extend shelf life.
Storage: Vacuum seal with oxygen absorber.

Sweet & Spicy Nuts

Per batch:

- 2 cups almonds or cashews
- 2 Tbsp honey powder + 1 Tbsp water
- ¼ tsp cayenne
- ½ tsp cinnamon
- ½ tsp salt

To Make: Toss nuts with spice mix. Bake at 300°F for 20 minutes. Dehydrate 4–6 hours to crisp. **Tip:** Barter item during tough times. **Storage:** Pint jars with oxygen absorber.

Pumpkin Spice Snack Mix

Per quart:

- 2 cups Chex cereal
- ½ cup mixed nuts
- ½ cup dried cranberries or apple bits
- 1 Tbsp pumpkin pie spice
- 2 Tbsp maple sugar or honey powder + 1 Tbsp water

To Make: Mix and gently bake at 250°F for 15 minutes. Dehydrate 4–6 hours for crunch. **Storage:** Airtight jars or Mylar.

Tropical Fruit Jerky

Blend per tray:

- 1 cup pineapple rings
- ½ cup mango strips
- ½ cup banana slices
- ¼ cup coconut flakes

To Make: Dehydrate at 125–135°F for 10–14 hours. Rotate trays. Condition before sealing. **Shelf Life:** 12–18 months in ideal storage.

BONUS: Ranch Roasted Almonds

Per batch:

- 2 cups almonds
- 1 Tbsp buttermilk powder
- 1 tsp onion powder
- ½ tsp garlic powder
- ¼ tsp dill
- ¼ tsp salt

To Make: Toss with seasonings. Bake at 300°F for 20 minutes. Dehydrate 4–6 hours. **Storage:** Pint jars with desiccant.

BONUS: Zesty Tomato Kale Chips

Per batch (2 trays):

- 4 cups kale leaves, washed and stemmed
- 1 Tbsp tomato powder
- 1 Tbsp nutritional yeast
- ½ tsp garlic powder
- 1 Tbsp oil

To Make: Toss evenly. Spread on trays. Dehydrate at 125°F for 6–8 hours until brittle. **Tip:** Store gently in jars with padding and desiccant.

Snacks aren't just about food — they're about normalcy, morale, and a sense of routine. Having these on hand means even the toughest days still have small joys built in.

More Snacks

Recipe Name	Ingredients (per jar)	To Make
Maple Cinnamon Pecans	1 cup pecans, 1 Tbsp maple sugar, ½ tsp cinnamon, pinch of salt	Toss ingredients to coat. Bake at 300°F for 20 minutes, stirring halfway. Dehydrate until crisp. Cool, vacuum seal with oxygen absorber.
Savory Parmesan Cheese Crisps	1 cup shredded Parmesan, ½ tsp Italian herbs	Spoon 1 Tbsp mounds onto parchment. Bake at 375°F for 6–8 mins until golden. Optional: dehydrate for extra crispness. Store airtight with desiccant.
Coconut Cashew Clusters	½ cup toasted cashews, ½ cup coconut flakes, 1 Tbsp honey or maple powder	Mix and press into clumps. Bake at 325°F for 10–15 mins until golden. Cool completely and vacuum seal.
Tangy BBQ Sunflower Seeds	1 cup sunflower seeds, 1 tsp BBQ seasoning mix	Coat seeds evenly, roast at 300°F for 15–20 mins, stirring halfway. Cool fully and store in airtight jars with desiccant.
Peanut Butter Banana Bites	½ cup banana chips, 1 Tbsp powdered peanut butter, 1 tsp honey powder	Toss banana chips with powders until coated. Dehydrate if needed. Vacuum seal with oxygen absorber.
Lemon Ginger Energy Squares	½ cup oats, ¼ cup shredded coconut, 1 tsp powdered lemon juice, ½ tsp ginger powder, 2 Tbsp date or honey powder	Mix, press into ½-inch thick layer, cut into squares. Dehydrate until firm. Store sealed in jars.
Pizza Snack Crackers	Homemade dough with 1 cup flour, 1 Tbsp tomato powder, 1 tsp oregano, ½ tsp garlic powder, 2 Tbsp cheese powder	Roll thin, cut, bake at 350°F for 12–15 mins, dehydrate fully. Store vacuum sealed.

Name	Ingredients	Instructions
Dill Pickle Popcorn Mix	3 cups air-popped popcorn, ½ tsp dill, ¼ tsp garlic powder, ¼ tsp vinegar powder, ½ tsp butter powder	Toss with seasonings, let cool fully. Store in dry jars with desiccant to retain crispness.
Chili Lime Corn Nuts	1 cup roasted corn kernels, ½ tsp chili powder, ½ tsp lime zest	Toss and roast at 325°F for 15–20 mins until crunchy. Cool completely and seal airtight.
Crispy Chickpea Trail Mix	½ cup roasted chickpeas, 2 Tbsp dried cranberries, 2 Tbsp pumpkin seeds, 2 Tbsp chocolate chunks (optional in heat)	Mix and store in cool, dry jars. Add oxygen absorber. Keep chocolate out in warm conditions.
Chocolate Mint Protein Bites	½ cup oat powder, 1 Tbsp cocoa, ¼ tsp mint powder, 2 Tbsp protein powder, 2 Tbsp nut butter powder	Mix, form into balls. Dehydrate until dry to touch. Vacuum seal in jars.
Everything Bagel Seed Mix	1 Tbsp sesame seeds, 1 Tbsp poppy seeds, 1 tsp onion flakes, 1 tsp garlic granules, ½ tsp salt	Toast seeds in dry skillet for 2 mins. Cool and store in airtight jars. Use as snack or topping.
Spiced Apple Walnut Bark	½ cup dehydrated apple slices, 1 Tbsp maple powder, ½ tsp cinnamon, 2 Tbsp chopped walnuts	Toss together and press into bark on tray. Dry thoroughly in dehydrator. Store airtight.
Carrot Cake Snack Bites	¼ cup dried shredded carrot, ¼ cup oats, ¼ tsp cinnamon, pinch nutmeg, 1 Tbsp raisins, 1 Tbsp shredded coconut, 1 Tbsp cream cheese powder	Mix, press into balls or bars. Dehydrate until firm and dry. Store vacuum sealed.
Crispy Rice Cereal Bites	1 cup puffed rice, 2 Tbsp honey powder, 2 Tbsp peanut butter powder, ¼ tsp vanilla powder	Mix, press into bars. Bake at 300°F or dehydrate until crisp. Store in airtight jars.

CHAPTER 9: DESSERTS

Sweet Comforts in Tough Times

Dessert might not be essential for survival, but it's absolutely essential for morale. When you've had a long day — whether from putting up firewood, dealing with uncertainty, or just living life off the grid — there's nothing like the comfort of a warm, homemade dessert. These jar-ready recipes make that possible with just a splash of water and a little heat.

Stored properly, these mixes can sit on a shelf for years, waiting for the day you want to surprise the kids or just bring a little sweetness to a hard week. And they're not just for emergencies — I make many of these on regular evenings, especially when we've got guests or are celebrating small blessings.

Chocolate Chip Cookie Mix

Per wide-mouth pint jar:

- ¾ cup all-purpose flour
- ¼ cup brown sugar
- ¼ cup white sugar
- ¼ tsp salt
- ¼ tsp baking soda
- ¼ cup chocolate chips

To Make: Mix jar contents with 1 egg and ¼ cup melted butter or oil (or ¼ cup water + 1 Tbsp powdered egg and 2 Tbsp oil). Drop spoonfuls on a baking sheet. Bake at 350°F for 10–12 minutes until golden brown.

Instant Apple Crisp

Per pint jar:

- ½ cup quick oats
- ¼ cup brown sugar
- ¼ tsp cinnamon
- 2 Tbsp powdered butter
- ½ cup freeze-dried apple slices

To Make: Add about ½ cup hot water, stir until moistened, and let sit 10 minutes. For best texture, bake at 350°F for 10–15 minutes or toast in a skillet until crisp on top.

Brownie Batter in a Jar

Per pint jar:

- ½ cup all-purpose flour
- ¼ cup cocoa powder
- ½ cup sugar
- 1 Tbsp powdered egg
- 2 Tbsp powdered milk
- ½ tsp instant coffee (optional)
- Pinch of salt

To Make: Add ¼–⅓ cup water, stir until thick like batter. Bake at 350°F for 20–25 minutes, or pan-cook covered until center sets. For a quick version, microwave in a mug for 90 seconds.

Cinnamon Rice Pudding

Per pint jar:

- ½ cup instant white rice
- 2 Tbsp powdered milk
- 1 Tbsp sugar
- ¼ tsp cinnamon
- 1 Tbsp raisins

To Make: Add 1 cup boiling water, stir well, and cover. Let sit 10–15 minutes. Stir again before serving. Add a dash of nutmeg or vanilla powder for extra richness.

Strawberry Shortcake Mix

Per pint jar:

- ¾ cup biscuit mix
- ¼ cup freeze-dried strawberries
- 1 Tbsp sugar

To Make: Rehydrate strawberries with 2–3 Tbsp water. Add ⅓ cup water to biscuit mix, stir, and drop spoonfuls on skillet or bake at 375°F for 12–15 minutes. Layer shortcakes with berries and a little honey if desired.

Peach Cobbler

Per pint jar:

- ½ cup powdered yellow cake mix
- 1 Tbsp sugar
- ¼ tsp cinnamon
- ½ cup freeze-dried peach slices

To Make: Mix contents with ½ cup water until thick. Bake in greased pan or pan-cook covered on low heat until set and golden.

Pumpkin Pie Spice Cake

Per pint jar:

- ½ cup all-purpose flour
- ¼ cup powdered pumpkin
- ¼ cup sugar
- 1 Tbsp powdered milk
- ¼ tsp cinnamon
- ¼ tsp nutmeg
- ⅛ tsp ginger
- ¼ tsp baking soda

To Make: Add ¼–⅓ cup water and mix well. Bake at 350°F for 20–25 minutes, or microwave as a mug cake for 90 seconds. Serve with a drizzle of honey or sprinkle of sugar.

Banana Bread Mix

Per pint jar:

- ¾ cup flour
- ¼ cup sugar
- 2 Tbsp powdered banana
- 1 Tbsp powdered milk
- 1 Tbsp powdered egg
- ¼ tsp baking soda

- ¼ tsp cinnamon

To Make: Add ⅓ cup water, mix gently. Pour into greased muffin tin or small pan. Bake at 350°F for 18–22 minutes or until toothpick comes out clean.

Blueberry Muffin Mix

Per pint jar:

- ¾ cup all-purpose flour
- ¼ cup sugar
- 1 tsp baking powder
- 1 Tbsp powdered egg
- 1 Tbsp powdered milk
- ¼ cup freeze-dried blueberries

To Make: Add ⅓ cup water, stir gently (don't overmix). Spoon into greased muffin tins. Bake at 375°F for 15–18 minutes.

S'mores Cake Mix

Per pint jar:

- ½ cup chocolate cake mix
- 2 Tbsp crushed graham crackers
- 2 Tbsp mini marshmallows
- 1 Tbsp sugar

To Make: Add ¼ cup water and stir to make a thick batter. Bake at 350°F or microwave for 90 seconds. If possible, toast the top for a true s'mores experience.

BONUS: Carrot Cake Pudding

Per pint jar:

- 2 Tbsp powdered carrot
- ¼ cup quick oats or flour
- 2 Tbsp sugar
- ¼ tsp cinnamon
- Pinch of nutmeg
- 1 Tbsp powdered milk
- 1 Tbsp raisins

To Make: Add ½ cup hot water. Stir and let sit 10 minutes, or heat gently in a pan until thickened. Optional: stir in a spoonful of honey or top with nuts.

BONUS: Lemon Poppy Seed Mug Cake

Per pint jar:

- ½ cup flour
- ¼ cup sugar
- 1 Tbsp lemon zest powder
- ½ tsp poppy seeds
- 1 Tbsp powdered egg
- 1 Tbsp powdered milk
- ¼ tsp baking soda

To Make: Add ¼–⅓ cup water and stir until smooth. Microwave in a mug for 90 seconds or steam in a covered dish for 15 minutes. Light, bright, and perfect for spring.

A well-stocked pantry doesn't just feed the body — it comforts the soul. These desserts are a reminder that even in hardship, we can still enjoy life's simple pleasures. Keep a few sweet jars tucked away, and you'll always have a reason to celebrate.

More Desserts

Recipe Name	Ingredients (per jar)	To Make
Maple Walnut Blondie Mix	½ cup flour, 2 Tbsp brown sugar, 1 Tbsp maple sugar, ¼ tsp baking soda, 1 Tbsp powdered egg, 2 Tbsp chopped walnuts	Add 3–4 Tbsp water. Stir to form thick batter. Spread in pan or mug. Bake at 350°F for 20–25 mins until golden.
Coconut Macaroon Bites	½ cup shredded coconut, 2 Tbsp sugar, 1 Tbsp powdered egg whites, pinch of salt	Add 2–3 Tbsp water, stir to form dough. Shape into mounds. Bake at 325°F for 12–15 mins or pan-toast on low heat until edges are crisp.
Gingerbread Mug Cake	¼ cup flour, 2 Tbsp brown sugar, ½ tsp ginger, ¼ tsp cinnamon, pinch of nutmeg, 1 tsp molasses powder, ¼ tsp baking soda, 1 Tbsp milk powder	Add 3 Tbsp water. Mix in mug. Microwave for 60–90 seconds or steam in cup until center is firm.
Raspberry Chocolate Crumble	¼ cup oats, 1 Tbsp sugar, 1 tsp cocoa powder, 1 Tbsp milk powder, 2 Tbsp freeze-dried raspberries, 1 Tbsp chocolate chunks	Add 3 Tbsp water. Stir and let sit 5 mins. Bake at 350°F for 10 mins or toast gently in skillet.
Lemon Bar Crumble	¼ cup flour, 2 Tbsp sugar, 1 tsp powdered lemon juice, 1 Tbsp milk powder, 2 Tbsp oat crumble topping	Mix with 3–4 Tbsp water. Layer in greased baking dish. Bake at 350°F for 20–25 minutes until golden.
Pineapple Upside-Down Mug Cake	¼ cup cake mix, 1 tsp brown sugar, 1 tsp powdered butter, 2 Tbsp freeze-dried pineapple	Add 3 Tbsp water, mix in mug. Microwave 60–90 seconds or steam

		covered. Let cool slightly before serving.
Cherry Almond Crumble	¼ cup oats, 1 Tbsp brown sugar, 1 Tbsp milk powder, pinch cinnamon, 2 Tbsp freeze-dried cherries, 1 Tbsp slivered almonds	Add ¼ cup hot water. Stir and let sit 5–10 mins. For crunch, bake at 350°F for 10 minutes.
Chocolate Pudding Mix	2 Tbsp cocoa, 2 Tbsp sugar, 1 Tbsp cornstarch, 2 Tbsp milk powder, pinch salt	Whisk into ¾ cup hot water. Simmer gently 5–7 mins until thickened. Stir frequently to avoid clumps.
Snickerdoodle Cookie Mix	½ cup flour, 2 Tbsp sugar, ¼ tsp cinnamon, ¼ tsp baking soda, 1 Tbsp milk powder, 1 Tbsp egg powder	Add 3 Tbsp water. Stir into dough, shape balls, roll in cinnamon sugar if desired. Bake at 350°F for 10–12 mins.
Mocha Cake in a Jar	2 Tbsp cocoa powder, 1 tsp instant coffee, ¼ cup flour, 2 Tbsp sugar, 1 Tbsp milk powder, 1 Tbsp egg powder, pinch cinnamon	Add 3 Tbsp water. Mix in jar or mug. Microwave 90 seconds or bake at 350°F for 20 mins.
Apple Cinnamon Muffin Mix	½ cup flour, 2 Tbsp sugar, 1 Tbsp powdered apple, ¼ tsp cinnamon, ½ tsp baking powder, 1 Tbsp milk powder, 1 Tbsp egg powder	Add 3–4 Tbsp water. Mix and spoon into muffin tin or skillet. Bake at 350°F for 18–20 mins.
Almond Joy Cookie Mix	2 Tbsp shredded coconut, 1 Tbsp mini chocolate chips, 1 Tbsp almond slivers, 2 Tbsp sugar, ¼ cup flour, 1 Tbsp milk powder, 1 Tbsp egg powder	Add 3 Tbsp water. Stir, shape into cookies. Bake at 350°F or skillet-cook over low heat.
Peanut Butter Mug Fudge	2 Tbsp peanut butter powder, 1 Tbsp cocoa, 1 Tbsp sugar, 2 Tbsp milk powder, pinch of salt	Add 2–3 Tbsp water. Mix in mug, microwave 30–60 seconds or steam for a dense, soft fudge.
Molasses Spice Biscuit Mix	½ cup flour, 1 Tbsp sugar, 1 tsp molasses powder, ¼ tsp ginger, ¼ tsp cinnamon, ¼ tsp baking soda	Add 3 Tbsp water. Stir, drop spoonfuls onto skillet or bake at 375°F for 10–12 minutes until firm and chewy.
Strawberries & Cream Rice Bake	¼ cup instant rice, 2 Tbsp milk powder, 1 Tbsp sugar, ½ tsp vanilla powder, 2 Tbsp freeze-dried strawberries	Add 1 cup hot water. Stir and let sit 10 minutes or simmer on stove until creamy and tender. Stir before serving.

CHAPTER 10: ADVANCED TIPS AND TRICKS

Once you've got the basics down, it's time to start tailoring your meals to fit your family's specific needs and lifestyle. These tips will help you avoid the pitfalls, stretch your resources, and even turn your jars into blessings for others. This isn't just about survival — it's about thriving with wisdom and grace, no matter what comes your way.

Customizing for Dietary Needs

Gluten-Free: Use certified gluten-free oats, rice pasta, or quinoa. Be careful with seasoning blends and bouillon — many contain hidden wheat. I always pack these jars on separate prep days and label them clearly to avoid cross-contamination.

Vegetarian or Vegan: Leave out meat and dairy powders, and focus on protein-rich legumes, grains, and seeds. Nutritional yeast is a great flavor booster, and coconut milk powder is an excellent vegan substitute for cream.

Low-Carb: Use cauliflower rice, freeze-dried broccoli, or green beans in place of traditional starches. Watch sugar content in snacks and desserts — substitute with monk fruit or stevia blends.

Allergies: Label every jar with potential allergens. I keep a color-coded label system — red for gluten, blue for dairy, green for nuts. It's simple and effective.

Scaling Recipes: For Families or Singles

The beauty of this system is flexibility.

For Larger Families: Use half-gallon jars or Mylar bags with 4–6 servings. I like to store bulk recipes in 5-gallon buckets with gamma lids, then fill jars weekly for ease of use.

For Singles or Couples: Pint jars work beautifully. Divide large batches into smaller containers. These are great for grandparents, college students, or folks living solo but wanting security.

Tip: Create a variety pack of single-serve jars to keep in the car, camper, or work truck.

Common Mistakes and How to Avoid Them

- **Using moisture-heavy ingredients:** Even slightly under-dried veggies can ruin a whole jar. Always test dryness before sealing.
- **Overfilling jars:** Leave a little headspace so the vacuum seal can properly engage. Tightly packed jars often lose seal over time.
- **Improper layering:** Powdery ingredients at the bottom trap moisture and can cake. Always layer powders near the top.
- **Skipping the oxygen absorber:** Don't rely on vacuum alone for long-term storage. OAs are critical.
- **Forgetting the label:** Trust me, once you've had to guess if a jar is chicken curry or lentil stew, you'll never forget to label again.

Creative Non-Emergency Uses

Meals in a jar are practical — but they're also delightful.

- **Gifts:** Tie a fabric square over the lid, add a tag with cooking instructions, and you've got a thoughtful gift for a new mom, neighbor, or friend in need.
- **Road Trips and Camping:** These jars have fed us on many a backwoods trip when the only heat source was a single-burner stove. Just add water and you're set.
- **Meal Prep:** When the week is busy, we use these as weeknight backups. Saves time and sanity.
- **Bartering and Blessing:** A shelf full of meals is also a way to bless others — especially in lean times. I keep a box of "extras" by the front door just in case someone needs a little help.

With a little creativity and discipline, your jars become more than food — they become a resource, a ministry, and a symbol of care and foresight.

CHAPTER 11: MEAL PLANNING AND ORGANIZATION

A shelf full of jars looks impressive, but real security comes from knowing *exactly what you have* and *how long it will last.* Proper planning and inventory management turn a stack of food into a well-oiled, resilient system — one that feeds your family not just today, but for months or years to come.

Let's break it down so you can build a pantry that serves your lifestyle, space, and budget.

How Much Food to Store

When calculating how much to store, I always go back to the basics: calories, protein, and frequency.

Daily Rule of Thumb (Per Adult):

- 1 Breakfast jar
- 1 Lunch jar or soup mix
- 1 Dinner jar
- 1 Snack or dessert

That's roughly **1,800–2,200 calories per day**, depending on portion size and ingredients. Children need slightly less, laborers need more.

Weekly Totals (Per Adult):

- 7 breakfasts

- 7 lunches
- 7 dinners
- 5–10 snacks/desserts

Monthly Totals (Per Family of 4):

- 30 breakfast jars
- 30 lunch jars
- 30–40 dinner jars (include some extras for guests or long days)
- 30+ snacks/desserts

Scale up or down based on your family size. I keep a laminated chart on our pantry door to help track these numbers.

Sample Monthly and Seasonal Meal Plans

To keep meals varied and spirits high, I rotate our meals seasonally. Here's a rough guide:

Spring/Summer Favorites:

- Lighter meals like veggie pilafs, quinoa bowls, fruit crisps, cold oatmeal jars.
- More cold snacks: trail mix, fruit jerky, granola.

Fall/Winter Staples:

- Hearty stews, chowders, curries, and warm puddings.
- Extra fats and protein to fuel colder days.

Sample Weekly Plan (Summer):

- Mon: Blueberry Oatmeal / Taco Soup / Pasta Primavera
- Tue: Pancake Mix / Tomato Soup / Chicken Curry
- Wed: Granola Parfait / Lentil Chili / Stroganoff
- Thu: Oatmeal / Minestrone / Fried Rice
- Fri: Grits & Sausage / Mac & Cheese / Chicken Alfredo
- Sat: Eggs & Bacon / Pilaf / Turkey Pot Pie
- Sun: French Toast Casserole / Barley Soup / Spaghetti & Meat Sauce

Organizing in Small Spaces

Not everyone has a root cellar or basement — and that's okay. Here's what I've seen work:

- **Closets:** Use labeled stackable crates or boxes.

- **Under Beds:** Slide totes or flat storage bins beneath bed frames.
- **Furniture Storage:** Ottomans, benches, or footlockers can double as storage.
- **Shelving in Garages or Sheds:** Just monitor temps — keep jars under 75°F and out of sunlight.

Remember: **cool, dark, and dry** are your guiding principles.

Building a Rotating Inventory

The key to making this system sustainable is regular rotation. Here's what we do:

1. **Label every jar** with date and meal name.
2. **Use oldest first** — work jars into your weekly meals, even during normal life.
3. **Restock seasonally** — every spring and fall, I spend a weekend assessing and refilling.
4. **Track usage** — a simple notebook or spreadsheet will do. I update mine monthly.

I also make a point to test one old jar a month — not just for rotation, but for confidence in the system.

Bonus Worksheets

Included at the end of this book are printable worksheets to help you:

- Track meal inventory by type and date
- Calculate meals per person per month
- Plan seasonal menus
- Set long-term food storage goals

Whether you're stocking a studio apartment or a full pantry room, these tools help you stay intentional, frugal, and prepared. A well-planned pantry is more than food. It's freedom. It's stewardship. It's a reflection of your care for the people you love.

CHAPTER 12: FREQUENTLY ASKED QUESTIONS

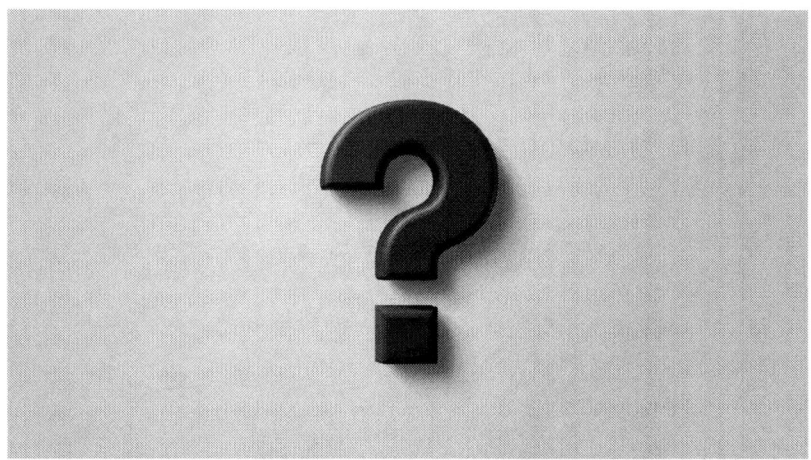

Even after years of putting up meals in jars, I still get questions — and still ask a few myself now and then. Food storage can feel intimidating when you're getting started, but most of the answers come down to careful observation, common sense, and a little good training.

Here are the questions I get most often — and the answers I've lived by.

How do I know it's still safe to eat?

This is one of the most important questions you can ask — and the answer comes down to using your **senses and sound judgment**.

Before opening the jar:

- Check the lid — is it still tightly sealed?
- Look for bulging lids, corrosion, or moisture inside. These are red flags.

After opening:

- Listen for the vacuum "pop." That sound is your first sign the seal held.
- Smell the contents — if anything smells musty, sour, rancid, or "off," discard it.
- Look for clumps, discoloration, or insect activity.

If you're unsure — *don't risk it.* Food security is about safety, not just storage.

What's the difference between freeze-dried and dehydrated?

Both remove moisture, but they do it differently — and it matters when you're planning for long-term meals.

- **Freeze-Dried:** Frozen first, then dried in a vacuum chamber. Light, crisp, retains shape and nutrients, rehydrates quickly. Shelf life: up to 25 years.
- **Dehydrated:** Uses warm air to slowly remove moisture. Denser, sometimes leathery or chewy, with shorter shelf life (5–10 years for most items).

When I use them:

- Freeze-dried for meats, fruits, and anything where texture matters.
- Dehydrated for soups, veggie blends, and anything going into a long simmer.

How much water do I need to add for each meal?

That depends on the ingredients, but here's a general guide:

- **Soups and Stews:** 1½ to 2 cups boiling water per ½ cup dry mix
- **Oatmeal/Grains:** ¾ to 1 cup water per ½ cup dry
- **Pasta Meals:** Add just enough to cover the pasta, then adjust
- **Instant meals (like granola parfaits or overnight oats):** ½ to ¾ cup water or milk

Each recipe in this book includes water instructions, but don't be afraid to tweak based on your taste. Keep notes. Over time, you'll learn exactly how your family likes it.

Can I safely use ingredients I dried at home?

Yes — with care and proper technique. I dehydrate most of our onions, peppers, tomatoes, and fruits myself. Here's what to watch for:

- **Dry completely:** Until crisp or leathery, with *no* visible moisture
- **Conditioning:** Store loosely for 5–7 days and shake daily to distribute moisture before sealing
- **Storage:** Use vacuum sealing with oxygen absorbers for best results

I always keep homemade dehydrated items for short- to mid-term storage (1–5 years), and rely on commercial freeze-dried for ultra-long-term meals.

What if I notice a broken seal?

Treat it seriously. If a lid flexes up and down or comes off easily, the vacuum is gone.

Check the contents:

- If dry, odor-free, and within 6–12 months of packing, it might be safe to use.
- If it smells off, has any clumping, or you see moisture — *discard immediately.*

When in doubt, I repurpose safe-looking contents into same-day meals, and I never re-seal food that's been exposed long-term. Always inspect seals *before* using. It only takes a second and could save you a whole lot of trouble.

CONCLUSION: ONE JAR AT A TIME

If you've made it this far, then I want you to hear me clearly: you are ready.

You don't need a professional kitchen, a thousand-dollar dehydrator, or every jar lid matching. You don't need permission. What you need is one quiet hour, one clean jar, and the faith to begin.

That first jar might feel clumsy. You'll second-guess the water-to-mix ratio. You'll wonder if your seal is tight enough or if your handwriting looks sloppy on the label. But here's the truth — none of that matters as much as the simple fact that you *did it*. That you took action. That you said, "I will feed my family, no matter what."

The first time I opened one of our early shelf meals in the middle of a power outage, I cried. Not because the meal was fancy — it wasn't. It was a jar of lentil stew. But it was *warm*. It was *ready*. It reminded me that all those quiet afternoons in the kitchen, all the planning and packing, were not in vain. I had prepared for this. And that's a kind of peace you can't buy.

Even a few jars lined up on a shelf can steady a household. They don't just hold food — they hold comfort. They hold resilience. They hold the love and effort you've poured in long before the need ever arrived.

Practical Wisdom to Carry With You

Label simply, but clearly.
Don't overcomplicate it. Use masking tape or sticky labels and a Sharpie. Write the meal name, the packing date, and brief cooking instructions. It's not about being fancy — it's about being functional.

Store your meals like they matter.
Cool, dark places are best — a basement, closet, or shaded pantry shelf. Avoid heat and light like the plague. A jar stored right is a jar that lasts.

Rotate and use what you've made.
Don't let your food gather dust. Build meals from your stockpile every week. This keeps your food fresh and helps you refine what recipes actually work for your family.

Make it more than a solo project.
Let your children scoop oats and seal jars. Invite a friend for a jar-packing afternoon. Send a jar to a neighbor who's hurting. This kind of preparedness isn't hoarding — it's hospitality.

This Isn't Just About Food

If all you got from this book was a list of recipes, then I've failed you. Because the deeper truth is this: preparedness is about freedom.

It's freedom from panic when storms roll in.
It's freedom from waste when you make every scrap count.
It's freedom from the weight of "what ifs" when you know your pantry is ready.

That's not fear. That's wisdom. That's stewardship. That's faith in action.

You'll save money.
No more spoiled lettuce or frantic store runs. No more drive-thru dinners because you forgot to thaw the meat. You'll cook from what you already have — and that's a blessing in more ways than one.

You'll be ready for hard seasons.
Job loss, inflation, sickness, even grief — they come whether we're ready or not. Having meals set aside means one less thing to worry about when your world feels shaky.

You'll build a home marked by steadiness.
Not isolation. Not fear. But quiet, faithful provision — the kind that grows with each jar you pack, each meal you make, and each child you teach.

So don't wait for things to calm down. Don't wait for the "right" time. Start now. Fill a jar. Label it with joy. Stack it on the shelf and smile, because you're doing it.

From my homestead to yours: may your shelves be full, your heart be steady, and your hands be blessed in the work ahead.